How to be an Alpha Male:
The 50 Rules of the Modern Day Alpha Male

D1785522

are for clarifying purposes only and are the owned by the owners themselves, not affiliated with this document.

Table Of Contents

Introduction

I want to thank you and congratulate you for downloading the book *How to be an Alpha Male.* If you are reading this book, most likely you are having trouble becoming the man you want to be. Perhaps you are sick of being stepped on, sick of feeling insignificant, and just had it up to here with everything. Maybe you keep losing the girl, or maybe you keep doubting yourself. Maybe you want a way to get stronger. Maybe you want a way to become the ultimate male. You know what I am talking about the alpha male...The one other males look to in times of crisis. The one everyone respects. The one who gets the girl and always succeeds. Yea, that one...

This book contains proven steps and strategies on how to become an alpha male. Becoming an alpha male can seem daunting at first, but trust me after reading this book you will have gained the confidence you need to succeed. This book will include sections discussing the importance of being an alpha male, characteristics of an alpha male, drawbacks that can cloud your judgement on your way to becoming an alpha male, 50 rules to follow and examples of how not to be an alpha male. So pretty much everything you need to know about becoming an alpha male.

Here's an inescapable fact: you will need dedication and confidence to become an alpha male. If you do not have the confidence now. It is not the end of the world. Confidence can be taught, and gained through experience and example. If you do not have the dedication, then you are lazy. Spoiler alert, alpha males are not lazy! To become determined and dedicated you need to have a fire burning within, a hunger so to speak. You need to have the passion to become the ultimate successor-an alpha male.

If you do not develop skills on how to be an alpha male. Don't give up! Alpha males are all about hard work and dedication. If they don't get something right away. Do you think they give up? NO! If they gave up, how would they succeed? How would they get the girl in the end? How would they be everything we aspire to today?

It's time for you to become an amazing alpha male. Don't take crap from anybody. Don't let people bring you down, and don't listen to what they say... This will be discussed further in the book, but I feel like I should say it now. Alpha males are not cowards, and they certainly do not let others bring them down, nor do they let others dictate what they say or do. An alpha male does what he wants and does so with the confidence of a million eagles soaring overhead.

Chapter 1: The Definition of an Alpha Male

What is an alpha male?

If you heard someone call another man an alpha male... What would you think? Do you have a clear picture in your mind of what makes an alpha male an alpha male? Do you imagine a man with broad shoulders, muscular, someone who doesn't play by the rules or someone who gets all the girls with a blink of an eye?

I don't know about you but that description sounds a little shallow. Is it me or was that entire description based on physicality and surely lacking in the mentality department? Sure physical aspects help make an alpha male, but it isn't the only thing that creates his inner strength.

Throughout the book we will discuss various characteristics of an alpha male and ways you too can become just as powerful and worldly. However, before we dive into that immense topic. Let me include the definition of an alpha male according to the internet. With a quick search of "alpha male" this description appears: "An alpha male has certain unmistakable characteristics. A natural leader, he is a pack builder. He leads, provides for and protects his pack (his significant other, his buddies, his teammates and so on)."

Sounds a little like a wolf? Or a dog? Well decades ago alpha males were found in the animal kingdom. So thinking back on to that definition it begins to make a little more sense. Let's travel back to the animal kingdom...

In the animal kingdom animals were always trying to become the alpha male. They wanted to be the one females wanted and loved. I believe chimpanzees started the cycle or perhaps it was an animal closer to the wolf family. I know dogs also have the tendency to find the alpha male in their relationships. Either way the concept of the alpha male began to evolve...and evolve...

Currently, animals are not just viewed as alpha males, but now humans to! A man wants to become an alpha male. He wants the strength, the respect and the courage. He wants to be more than just the provider, but someone who is confident in his own abilities. Someone who doesn't doubt himself. Someone who is respected by both sexes. Someone who is able to stand up for himself. Someone who is able to walk a path entirely his own. Someone who can succeed because he believes he can. Someone who has the courage to make a difference. Someone who can express his emotions. Someone who has control of all his senses. Someone who can take on the world.

This is what an alpha male is to me. He is a man, and not a cowardice boy. He is someone you can depend on. Someone you can love. Someone you can trust.

An alpha male is more than just all those characteristics. He is the embodiment of them. He is the passion that is created from within.

Chapter 2: Why Alpha Males Succeed in Life

What makes them so special?

I am sure you have looked at a man once and wondered... How did he get where he is today? No? You haven't... I find that highly unlikely. People watching is very common all over the world. The curiosity that yearns for an answer is always within us. So admit it. You have watched people and wondered how they have become who they are.

Maybe you have even gotten jealous, wondering... Why can't you be just as successful? Sometimes you will try to bargain with yourself and say...He was born with it or he is just rich... 9 times out of 10 that really isn't the truth. It makes us feel better though, doesn't it? We try not to blame ourselves for our current situation, and find a better excuse instead. An excuse we begin to use throughout more of our lives.

Stop making excuses! You can become just as successful! You can become the alpha male... Doubting yourself and making up excuses is just one of the many examples of how not to be an alpha male. (I will have an entire chapter towards the end dedicated to that topic, so I will only mention it briefly here.)

Let us break down the concept of success. What is truly the definition? Well with a quick search on the internet the definition is: "the accomplishment of an aim or purpose. The attainment of popularity or profit. A person or thing that achieves desired aims or attains prosperity." Hmm looking through those definitions I would argue the last one will better suite our needs.

Let us break down how alpha males gain that success... To understand the how we need to understand the who... Simply meaning, let us discuss more characteristics of the alpha male that allow advancement in our society and ultimately accomplishment.

Alpha males succeed in life because they know who they are. They don't need to find themselves with trial and error, because they already did. They didn't become who they are today with pure luck. They made it happen. They had that drive. They knew what they wanted out of life and grabbed it by the balls. This determination allows them the drive to continue and this leads to success. An alpha male will not give up as easily, and will not make excuses for his mistakes.

Alpha males are also confident. They don't need to listen to what other people say about them nor do they have any desire to do so. They are confident in their abilities, and rarely ever have doubt. They are confident in their decisions and rarely ask for approval. Because an alpha male is confident, he doesn't seek approval from others, and he doesn't let others negativity bring him down.

Alpha males usually do things on their own terms. They go their own path. Or as Robert Frost said "Two roads diverged in a wood and I- I took the one less traveled by." Alpha males will have success, but by their own terms. They will find a unique approach and follow through. Others may see this approach as foolish, but alpha males pay no attention to negativity. They are comfortable with who they are and their decisions.

Those are just a few of the characteristics of an alpha male in terms of success. To be successful is obviously high on the list when you are an alpha male. Success is gained through experience and dedication. Two things alpha males have gained over time...

Chapter 3: Why Alpha Males Always Get the Girl
It just doesn't seem fair...

It seems they always get the girl...But how? Why do girls tend to fall for alpha males over other men? Some would probably chuckle at this point, and simply say, because alpha males are well, alpha. They are better in every way, and of course nice guys always finish last...

Enough with your excuses. Newsflash, alpha males can also be nice, in fact that is one of the characteristics that make them so irresistible to women. Being nice is not a fault, but in fact a huge advantage.

Most women become attracted to an alpha male because of what he contributes to the relationship. His confident is a huge positive. Women like to know their man is confident and that he is strong. Also throughout the relationship, that confidence could rub off on the woman. A woman likes to know that the man is confidence in the relationship and believes in it. An alpha male does just that. A woman feels less hesitation over the relationship.

Most women adore that an alpha male has control over his emotions and is able to easily express himself. He is not afraid or emotionally closed off. He is open to his woman, and allows communication to flourish in the relationship.

Women like to be with a leader. They like to be with someone in charge. An alpha male takes control and is a role model in some aspects. Women feel special when they get to be with someone of those qualities. They feel like they hit the jackpot, because they know he will always be there.

Women like that alpha males are a provider and protector to them. An alpha male is able to easily provide for his woman. He protects his woman from hurt and allows her to feel wanted. Women like to feel wanted and needed. It is common knowledge.

An alpha male also tends to put his woman on a pedestal. He does not take his woman for granted nor does he play mind games with her. He does not lead her on, or confuse her with lies. An alpha male has nothing to hide. He shows his love and is able to connect in the relationship.

An alpha male will also spend more time listening then speaking. A woman loves to be heard, especially if she has had a rough day. Women gravitate towards someone who can be there for them. An alpha male is a true leader and will never leave her side. He will listen to his woman, give his opinion, and let her express herself. He is not afraid of her emotions because he is not afraid of his.

Women also love a man who is fit. Most alpha males are fit and have joined a gym. Becoming an alpha male comes from inside, but if you feel good on the outside then your inside will feel the same in no time. Another reason why staying fit is a must... is because it shows you are taking care of yourself. It shows you can take care of others as well. Simply meaning, you can provide and protect for them.

Women also love a man who can dress well. Alpha males tend to dress better than other men. They like to stick out, because they have the confidence to pull it off. Alpha males may wear a patterned or collared shirt to show individuality.

Another thing an alpha male does that attracts women is...flirt. Alpha males are experienced and have superb flirting skills. They are able to make a connection easily, and keep it. I would argue this goes back to their ability to express their emotions.

There are numerous reasons why women fall for the alpha male, but the one you really need to keep in mind is.... Women love a man who is confident and has the ability to express himself. A woman is never left guessing when she is in the company of an alpha male.

Chapter 4: How Seeking Others Approval Will Ruin Your Life
I just want to be liked...

I know everyone wants to be liked, but when you are an alpha male it is the furthest thing from your mind. You have the confidence to do what you want and what you feel is best. You are not stuck in the one track mind of seeking approval from everyone you meet.

Most men bend over backwards to seek approval. Actually I think everyone does. Both women and men. We all just want to be liked. Is it really that bad?

Well from an alpha male's perspective, yes that is wrong. Alpha males do not need approval from anyone. They make their own luck and run their own life. They have the confidence to live the way they want to. They do not allow others to run their life nor do they give others the upper hand.

They are strong leaders who don't rely on anyone but themselves. Possibly they have been let down before, so they don't include others' opinions in their mind.

Let's break down the situation shall we... Why are you seeking approval??

If you are always seeking approval, then you must not feel confident in your own abilities. If you are always asking "Is this ok?"... You must not feel like you are enough, or what you are doing is not enough. An alpha male doesn't have thoughts of those nature. His thoughts are more towards improving his position in life. He knows that he can always do better, and is not afraid to go for it!

An alpha male never allows negativity to cloud his judgement. He knows his abilities and has the confidence to succeed. If you always seeking approval, then you are not believing in yourself. This meaning you do not have the confidence. Maybe you are trying to get the confidence from someone else, or you are trying to let someone else control you.

Remember an alpha male claims control and is a true born leader. He doesn't allow other people to control him or his decisions. The only approval he seeks is the approval of himself. Is he happy with himself? Has he done all he can to better himself? How can he help others the way he has helped himself?

An alpha male is always wanting to learn more and acquire new skills. He wants to help others accomplish their goals as well.

The next chapter coincides wonderfully with this one...It is important not to seek approval, but also important not to care what others say.

Chapter 5: Stop Caring What Others Say
But he said that....

I know it is only human to care what others say of you, but to be an alpha male-you need to go beyond the realm of humanity. You can't let little things like that bother you. You can't let other people tell you what to do or say...You are in control of your emotions and your ability. Don't let others stop you from succeeding.

If you care what others think and/or say about you... You are giving them the power. An alpha male is powerful, but not egotistical. He will not boast of his achievements or claim to be something that he is not. An alpha male allows others to see him for how he really is, and that is it. No fancy foot work, no fancy ways of getting around the inevitable, but just pure honesty.

An alpha male is honest in all things he does and says. He doesn't put on a show for others or cares how others perceive him. He knows what he is doing is right and doesn't need someone to tell him how to act.

An alpha male makes his mark in the world. Sounds like a dog marking his territory, and it is similar to that reference as well. An alpha male will make sure that he uses his presence as more than a gesture, but as a gateway to communication.

He will fill up the room with his strong posture, extensive gestures and yet look relaxed and comfortable. He will give specific body language that will convey his approach to his superiors.

He will use his eyes as a way to communicate when all else fails. His eyes will be very powerful, and strong. There may even be a hint of mystery within him. As already discussed, an alpha male is onderful listener. So he may listen to what you say, but that doesn't' mean he will agree with it, or even change his ways because of it.

An alpha male is polite in all things he does. He will not cause a scene nor find pleasure in gossip/or drama. Remember, an alpha male is a real man, and not a fragile little boy.

An alpha male is more than what meets the eye.

 The next chapter will focus on the 50 rules of an alpha male. Hopefully these will put into perspective, just what an alpha male represents and how to keep the illusion forever alive.

Chapter 6: 50 Rules of an Alpha Male
So many rules...

We have actually already discussed a few of the rules in the beginning of the book. I will still review them so you are confident in your abilities of becoming an alpha male. Are you ready? If you were an alpha male you would have said yes right away, and not even have a doubt in your mind towards the question....

1) An alpha male must be confident. I know this rule has been stated, and maybe even over stated throughout the book. However, don't confuse arrogance with confidence. These are two very different things! Arrogance gives the perception of an insecure man, but confidence gives the perception of a strong man.

2) An alpha male must assume a position. He walks into the room and has everyone's eyes on him. He gets the respect he deserves.

3) An alpha male must use humor to his advantage. He is not afraid to laugh at himself, and show his humility.

4) An alpha male must let his body do the talking. His body language will be prominent and strong. He will not slouch, but instead stand tall.

5) An alpha male must fill the room with his presence. He will use strong posture, gestures and the use of his eyes.

6) An alpha male must spend more time listening than speaking. He will respond better with people.

7) An alpha male must watch others. He will learn how to be a better alpha male, by observing other alpha males.

8) An alpha male must join a gym and stay fit. He will show can take care of himself as well as others.

9) An alpha male must be honest. He will not trick or deceive.

10) An alpha male must dress well. He will dress in a unique way to get others attention.

11) An alpha male must learn how to flirt. Flirting opens up the pathways to a romantic connection.

12) An alpha male must have the desire to develop new skills. Learning new skills allows your body to remain sharp and in shape.

13) An alpha male must be a leader. He needs to take charge of a situation and do it well.

14) An alpha male must be comfortable with himself. This goes along with the rule of being confident.

15) An alpha male must be passionate about life. He knows what he wants to do and is ready to go get it.

16) An alpha male must be able to bounce back after a failure. He will acknowledge it, but know he can learn from the experience.

17) An alpha male is always composed. He won't allow minor things to unnerve him.

18) An alpha male must be driven. He must have the dedication to succeed.

19) An alpha male must have high morals and values. He must know who he is and what he values in life.

20) An alpha male must believe in growth. He must know that he can change and progress.

21) An alpha male must not be bossy. He likes to let everyone share their ideas.

22) An alpha male must know that he doesn't have to prove himself. This goes along with not seeking approval from others.

23) An alpha male must be clever. He should know how to get out of situations and use his reasoning.

24) An alpha male must be dominant. He must possess prodigious social skills.

25) An alpha male must hang out with other alpha males. This goes along with the rule of observing others.

26) An alpha male must remain optimistic. He will always see the positive side of things.

27) An alpha male must talk slowly. He will not rush things.

28) An alpha male must walk slowly. He will be disciplined and relaxed.

29) An alpha male must be very good with communication. He is able to express himself.

30) An alpha male must be witty. He will use his humor to make light of the situation.

31) An alpha male must know that he is important. He will rely on himself.

32) An alpha male must demonstrate strength. He must show he can be a provider and protector.

33) An alpha male must be persistent. He will not give up easily.

34) The alpha male must be able to defend himself and his family.

35) The alpha male must be courageous. He accepts fear, knows it exists, and wants to face it.

36) The alpha male must be able to entertain.

37) The alpha male must be humble. He will never let himself get too big of an ego.

38) The alpha male must be educated. He should have an education, and a hunger for knowledge.

39) The alpha male must be a hard worker. He knows it takes time to accomplish great things.

40) The alpha male must be a warrior and not a worrier.

41) The alpha male must know how to treat a lady. He is chivalrous, and helps his lady reach her dreams.

42) The alpha male must not be a sucker. This meaning he will not go out of his way to please everyone.

43) The alpha male must help others.

44) The alpha male must be generous.

45) The alpha male must not try to be an alpha male. He lets it just happen on its own. He knows what he wants in life.

46) The alpha male must be tolerant of others and of his situation.

47) The alpha male must know the value of collaboration.

48) The alpha male must have initiative and start doing things, while other people are just waiting.

49) The alpha male must maintain his integrity.

50) The alpha male must never feel alone.

I hope those rules put it into perspective for you. Being an alpha male is more complicated than one would think. I am not saying it is hard to become one, but it takes dedication and hard work.

Chapter 7: How Not To Be an Alpha Male

So you are telling me I am doing it wrong?

Well if you just read through all the rules and do the opposite... That would be a simple way of figuring out what you are doing wrong. However, I will break it down into a few main common mistakes men make.

Mistake one: They are not confident. You cannot be an alpha male if you don't have any confidence! So gain that confidence and give it a go.

Mistake two: They are not expressive enough. If you can't share or control your emotions, then you can't be an alpha male.

Mistake three: They seek approval from others. An alpha male doesn't seek approval, but rather gives approval to others.

Mistake four: They care what other people say. An alpha male doesn't care what others say, and believes in himself.

Mistake five: They can't lead. You have to be a leader to be an alpha male.

Mistake six: They don't have the drive. You can't be an alpha male if you don't have the drive and dedication.

Mistake seven: They don't have the strength. You can't be an alpha male if you are weak, or have weak perceptions of the world.

Mistake eight: They rush everything. Alpha males take their time in life and decisions. They don't make rushed decisions.

Mistake nine: They are too egotistical. A true alpha male is humble in his approach and grace.

Mistake ten: They are afraid to fail. A real alpha male knows that failure is a healthy part of life. He knows he will bounce back and be able to succeed.

Those are just a few of the common mistakes men make. The first one is the most crucial. YOU NEED TO HAVE CONFIDENCE TO SUCCEED.

It is normal to make mistakes while on this journey of becoming an alpha male.

Conclusion

Thank you again for downloading this book! I hope this book has helped you on your journey of becoming an alpha male. I hope this book was able to push some misconceptions aside, and give you a clearer picture of the concept of an alpha male. Hopefully you have gained the inner strength and are able to be the top dog as some say, or whatever animal you want to be in the kingdom.

I hope this book was able to help you become confident in your abilities. Hopefully you have gained perspective and clarity with this book. Hopefully this book has opened up the doorways of communication and you are able to flourish. May your journey to becoming an alpha male be rewarding and ever changing.

The next step is to practice and learn by experience. Take those rules and apply them to your life. Most importantly make sure you have the confidence to succeed. If you still don't feel ready to give it a try, then observe other alpha males. By observance you will gain the confidence that you need to succeed. Gain the strength you need and never, ever, give up. Keep working at it, and one day... You will become the alpha male. You will become the dream that every man aspires to.

Finally, if you enjoyed this book, please take the time to share your thoughts and post a review on Amazon. It'd be greatly appreciated!

Thank you and good luck!

Printed in Great Britain
by Amazon